White Lion
Press

Tiny
essentials of
a fundraising
strategy

I would like to say a special thanks to Susan Robinson for her encouragement, insightful suggestions and all-around support throughout the project.

Ilene Hoyle

White Lion
Press

Tiny

essentials of
a fundraising
strategy

*by Maggie Taylor
and Ilene Hoyle*

Published by
The White Lion Press Limited
567 Ben Jonson House
The Barbican
London
EC2Y 8NH

© 2009 Ilene Hoyle/Helen Taylor/The White Lion
Press Limited
ISBN-13: 978-0-9553993-2-9
ISBN-10: 0-9553993-2-7

Cover photography by Neil Waterson

Other photography by Alan Clayton and Ernest
Muller

Design and print production by em associates

Printed and bound in the United Kingdom by Bell
& Bain Ltd, Glasgow

Contents

The authors

Maggie Taylor

Some years ago, when Ken Burnett was speaking at a fundraising seminar in Scotland, he took the opportunity to catch a presentation given by his old friend Maggie Taylor. Her session was on fundraising strategy and Ken was hugely impressed, not just by Maggie's enthusiasm and her presentation skills, but by the content of her workshop and the simplicity of her overall message. In fact, Maggie explained the fundamentals of such a strategy and how to go about preparing it so well that he persuaded her to write a Tiny book: *Tiny Essentials of a Fundraising Strategy*.

Sadly, Maggie died before she finished it, but fellow fundraising consultant and trainer Ilene Hoyle agreed to finish it as a tribute to her close friend. The work that she had started deserved to be finished and made available to fundraisers everywhere, as Maggie would have wished.

Maggie worked for many years as a dedicated fundraiser who understood the grass-roots issues that charities face. She went on to become a Fellow of the Institute of Fundraising as an accomplished trainer and mentor for many fundraisers and a first-class consultant.

Ilene Hoyle

Ilene Hoyle has been dedicated to the not-for-profit sector since she sold lemonade on her New York doorstep for the March of Dimes at the age of three. She officially joined the sector in the early 1980s in the UK, when she started a charity supporting the literacy needs of deaf people. Since then she has been a fundraiser for local, regional and national charities and a consultant and trainer in fundraising and governance since 1999.

Ilene is a passionate supporter of excellence in fundraising within smaller nonprofits. She is one of the accredited trainers and assessors who teach the Certificate of Fundraising across the UK for the Institute of Fundraising. In the interest of ensuring that fundraising is at the heart of nonprofits, she provides a comprehensive range of courses for boards of trustees on aspects of governance. More recently she has joined a small business network to promote high quality job recruitment in fundraising.

Preface

This little book tells you all you need to know about introducing, planning and implementing a strategy that's right for you and your organisation. What's more, it'll give you all this valuable insight and information in just about an hour, as that's all the time it will take you to read and digest this latest addition to the indispensable 'Tiny Essentials' series.

We stress this fact because our strategy is to recognise that your time is far too precious for you to lose too much of it tied up in reading long, impenetrable business books.

Of course it's hard to consider strategy without conjuring up military connotations, perhaps because the term derives from the Greek word for army. Strategy differs from tactics in that tactics are concerned with the conduct of a specific engagement while strategy is concerned with how different engagements are linked. In other words, how a battle is fought is a matter of tactics: whether it should be fought at all is a matter of strategy.

Equally, strategy is almost inseparable from the concept of leadership, for one without the other is unlikely to amount to much. That wily leader Winston Churchill once remarked, 'However beautiful the strategy, you should occasionally look at the results.' That, we feel, is a lesson worth learning, for implicit in it is the realisation that preparing your strategy is a beginning, not an end. And US General Norman Schwartzkopf said, 'Leadership is a potent combination of strategy and character. But if you must be without one, be without the strategy.'

Wise words, no doubt. But strategy is not about war, it's merely about winning. Former UN Secretary General Kofi Annan once said, 'There is no development strategy more beneficial to society as a whole – women and men alike – than the one which involves women as central players.'

Maggie Taylor and Ilene Hoyle would certainly agree with that. More importantly, here they show how, with a little foresight and application matched with planning and judicious engagement of all the players, it is possible to devise and implement an effective strategy without getting too hot and bothered about it in the process.

We hope you enjoy and benefit from this Tiny book.

x

Why should you have a fundraising strategy?

Fundraising without an effective strategy can be a scary experience. If you have been given a target and a deadline but no guidance about how these fit into your charity's overall plans, it can be like setting out on a journey into the unknown, on your own, without a map, local guidebooks, or companions to advise you. Lose your way, fail to get there and the consequences can be dire. Arrive at your destination safely, with time to spare and the benefits can be considerable.

Would you visit a place you've never been to before, without a map or a guide? The most likely answer is no, because if you did you might get lost and have no means of finding your way except for your own intuition. It's the same with fundraising. As management guru Charles Handy once wrote, 'If you don't know where you are going, all roads lead there.'

This is where a fundraising strategy comes in. It's the difference between the unplanned and the planned, the structured and the accidental.

Ownership

To illustrate, consider Rebecca, a fundraiser employed by a children's charity to raise £8 million. When asked how this target was arrived at, Rebecca shrugged her shoulders and said, 'I don't know, I wasn't included when the target was set and I wasn't included in the planning process.' And when asked if she could raise that amount of money, again she shrugged her shoulders and said, 'I don't think so.'

Any fundraiser who, like Rebecca, is divorced from planning and target setting is unlikely to feel engaged with or confident about the job she's expected to do. Rebecca needs a fundraising strategy she can own.

Instead, she has been given a target for how much she has to raise, but has not been shown either her organisation's overall business plan or its fundraising strategy. In fact she has no fundraising tools at all.

Not surprisingly, Rebecca thinks she might be in the wrong job.

Tony is the chief executive of a different organisation, the Phoenix Trust, a medium-sized healthcare charity he set up five years ago to support a minority group with a particularly debilitating genetic medical condition. He is clever and the charity has grown in size and influence. He has just appointed his first full-time fundraiser, Michael, who is equally bright.

During Michael's first day, Tony asked him how much he could raise. Michael's response was immediate, 'You asked me the wrong question. Tell me how much you and the Phoenix Trust *need* me to raise and I will tell you if I think it is possible, but only after we have worked together to put a fundraising strategy in place.'

Assembling the strategy

Fundraising is not only about money. It is also about the people – networks and contacts that an organisation can tap into – that in turn can lead to money that might be raised. Fundraisers are not magicians. They need the tools to do the job.

The framework, or strategy, for fundraising is essential. It is a plan that identifies the resources that will be needed to fund the work a nonprofit intends to do over three to five years, as identified in the organisation's overall business plan. All departmental plans, including the fundraising strategy, have to fit in with the business plan.

Fundraisers assemble their strategy based on information provided at many levels: by project officers, finance staff, or whoever makes decisions about the programme of work. After this strategy has been understood and agreed by the board of trustees, the fundraisers turn it into a detailed action plan to make it happen.

Michael already had experience in fundraising, through his work in the trusts and foundations fundraising team of a large national charity. In that role he had worked with several wise fundraisers and had seen the process involved in putting together the strategic plan for raising funds from trusts. Tony and the rest of the recruitment panel had seen this experience as a great asset.

The business plan

Michael was now ready to embark on his fundraising journey. But who was setting the aim (also known as purpose or goal) for his fundraising? Where was his strategy? He was the Trust's first fundraiser, so he suspected – correctly – that there was no fundraising strategy in place. He was aware that it wasn't his job to define where the organisation was going – setting the vision and the mission is the role of the board of trustees – but he did have to see the Phoenix Trust's plan to see how they had mapped the charity's direction over the next three to five years.

The business plan that Tony, his colleagues and the board had written was really helpful for Michael, and he felt greatly encouraged. The plan listed each project proposed for the next three years, alongside a clear expenditure and income budget for each project. The plan also identified how much of the overhead costs would be absorbed by each project. There were no extra 'core costs', as all costs, from insurances to cleaners, to the costs of governance and Tony's salary, were split across the projects. Because the business plan covered the current year and two years into the future, Michael was able to map out easily what funds were required this year, next year and the following year. That was the easy bit – now he had to raise this money, but without a fundraising strategy he felt he would be shadow boxing.

Michael had planned his career move carefully. His aim was to go from a job where he was part of a large team of fundraisers, each undertaking different roles in terms of raising income, to a smaller organisation where he would be in the driving seat – putting the fundraising systems in place, more or less from scratch. At the Phoenix Trust he would be running the whole fundraising function. To start with at least, he would *be* the fundraising department.

Without a fundraising strategy he would be shadow boxing

He had a month off between jobs and used this time to step back and take a look at what was going on in fundraising overall, so that he was prepared for his new post. During this time Michael worked hard to come up with a list of the important things he would do as fundraiser at the Trust.

Michael's list

1. Personal and career goal – to be the most learned fundraiser of my generation. Study fundraising history and current practice. Attend the best seminars around, consult the best books, magazines and websites about fundraising. In time, encourage all colleagues to do the same.

2. Promote a culture of best practice for the team at the Phoenix Trust. Gather as much information and materials as possible about the basics of good habits in fundraising, to use in the induction and support of new members to the future fundraising team at the Trust.

3. Create the best donor development strategy. Plan to start donor development at the Trust with the radical view that fundraisers should see everything they do from the point of view of the donor, so they offer donors what they want from the relationship, rather than what traditional donor development strategies dictate. Develop a culture of high quality donor service for all of the Trust's supporters and donors.

4. Focus upon strategies for long-term thinking and income, for instance committed giving and bequest income, rather than being driven by short-term targets.

5. Make sure the Phoenix Trust is a listening organisation. Develop a communications strategy that is not only effective and imaginative, but ensures that the Trust's fundraisers always listen with care to what donors and supporters tell them.

Talk to donors and actively involve them in seeing the tangible benefits of their support for the Trust. Take every opportunity to really understand the Trust's work; turn interest into a passion that will inspire and motivate donors to give.

These five principles, Michael decided, would be the cornerstones of his philosophy for fundraising. He was clear that they would be essential for him at the Phoenix Trust and throughout his fundraising career.

Some meetings are important

Armed with his principles, Michael met with Tony to discuss the Trust's business plan, specifically how to translate the business plan objectives for the next three years into a document that would highlight the overall fundraising needs of the Phoenix Trust.

He also had a meeting with the staff who deliver projects at the Trust, to find out their needs and to set fundraising objectives for each of the services identified in the plan. This, he felt, would help him identify any funding gaps in the Trust's current income. Clearly if the organisation did not have enough funds to meet its day-to-day operational needs, it would not have a future so there would be no point planning for it!

The challenges

One of Michael's challenges was to raise funds for the rent of a branch office. Another was to fund support for those people with MJS, the medical condition that the Trust existed to fight, who were losing income due to sporadic periods of illness. A third challenge was to raise money for the production and distribution of information sheets about the condition and its treatment. He decided that the strategy he was preparing would consider the kind of fundraising that would work for each of these projects and when the income was needed. Michael wanted to work on a 'total costs' basis. By working on pricing and costing with the finance officer at the Trust, he could be sure that his fundraising target figures took all costs into account, whether for insurance for the rented offices, or for the design costs of preparing the information sheets.

How the strategy might be achieved

Once the aim of the fundraising strategy was clear, Michael was able to set some objectives defining how it might be achieved. To do this, he needed to review the organisation's income over the last three years to see where it had come from. He already knew that the most common income sources were likely to be:

• Statutory income (from government departments, local and health authorities and other public bodies).

• Non-statutory income, from charitable trusts and foundations, the corporate sector (including large companies and small local businesses) and the general public (including one-off donations, regular gifts, direct mail appeals, events and legacies).

But what about earned income, or contracts, or possible partnerships as ways to bring in funds? Each of these elements would need to be looked into in more detail.

Michael then looked at the Trust's income within a seven-year time frame – the past three years, the current financial year and projections for the next three years. This gave him a real sense of his task. He could see clearly which sources of income were performing well and *increasing*, which were *static* and needed reviewing and which were *falling* or failing to perform and would need to be improved urgently or replaced.

Michael was also able to consider new areas of income that had never been tried before. Were there possible links with some of the pharmaceutical companies that provide the drugs used by beneficiaries? Could the Trust turn the oft-repeated praise for its work into a commodity and act as a consultant, advising other health authorities how to provide best practice? Most of the Trust's income had come from statutory funding, was it now time to consider fundraising from individuals, increasing the role of local people as volunteers, creating partnerships for fundraising? No time to daydream, he needed to arrange to talk to Tony and the project managers to see if these ideas would fit into the overall business plan.

Michael felt quite excited at the prospect of having a free rein to experiment with new approaches for fundraising, but he knew that he would have little money to invest in these activities. Therefore he needed to produce facts and figures to support the rationale for doing what he would be proposing. He also had to convince his board of trustees that they should, if necessary, raise the funds for this investment in the future of the charity. Perhaps they could help with fundraising from wealthy individuals, or open doors at that pharmaceutical company?

So, Michael was now ready for stage two of preparing the fundraising strategy – the case for support.

Learning points

1. Establish how the business plan underpins the fundraising strategy and identifies the need for funds for projects, services or activities.

2. Identify and quantify existing income sources. Categorise these into increasing, static and falling.

3. Quantify what you'll need to raise from new sources and create a preliminary list of what these new sources might be.

4. Consider the role of Michael's five cornerstones in your thinking and planning.

Your fundraising case

Packing for a holiday is usually a straightforward task, but it does need a little thought. What goes in your suitcase depends on the type of trip, the destination, the climate and why you have selected that holiday. Is it a week doing the galleries in Florence, skiing in the Alps, or basking by the ocean reading long novels? The contents of your fundraising suitcase will take a lot more thought, but this too will be dictated by your journey – where are you trying to get to and what route do you plan to take? Or rather, the types of fundraising you undertake will be determined by the nature of your organisation and how you describe the way you are solving the problem, meeting the need.

When Michael started his journey at the Phoenix Trust he asked to see all the publicity and printed materials available, so he could get a sense of how the Trust described itself and promoted its work. There wasn't much to be found. There were no good, compelling leaflets, no newsy, informative magazines, no striking posters, no website. He did find some information leaflets that were a great help to the people living with MJS but these wouldn't be any good at raising money. The only other publication was the annual report and accounts. It was pretty useless – long-winded, pompous, with no illustrations at all. There was no punchy strapline to let the world know what the Trust did, and no simple logo either. Effective fundraising would require both.

The case for support

Michael's fifth principle was to make the Phoenix Trust a listening organisation. It needed to produce communications that were effective and imaginative, and which showed it was listening carefully to *all* it's supporters. All it's communications had to be a dialogue between the Trust and its stakeholders. Obviously something had to be done – and fast – to help the Trust improve its communications.

Like any other organisation the Phoenix Trust has to project a positive image of itself and its work if it is to raise enough money to make a difference to people's lives. But before attempting to improve its fundraising materials, before tackling the issues of branding and the Trust's approach to publicising its work, Michael felt that his immediate priority was to prepare a clear, compelling and straight-forward statement that explained why donors should give to the Phoenix Trust, based on its achievements, values and requirements. This statement is known as *the case for support*. It's an essential fundraising tool, a core component of any fundraising strategy.

It's an essential fundraising tool…

Selling success

Michael needed to get to grips with what this meant in reality. How to convince donors to give their regular financial support – and lots of it – to the Phoenix Trust? When he asked members of staff for their opinions they all felt that even though the Trust was only five years old it had been extremely successful in supporting people with MJS. It has helped them to learn more about the condition so they can manage it and, despite its restrictions, live happy, productive and relatively trouble-free lives. The Trust helps them to develop regimes, not only to function effectively on a day-to-day basis, but also to adopt strategies for the medium- and, hopefully, the long-term future.

However, for many clients there will be no long term, as life expectancy for sufferers of MJS is often reduced. A fundraiser in this position has to be sensitive to this and not approach the subject like the grim reaper – all doom and gloom. The perspective has to be about enhancing and enriching the limited lifespan that many of the organisation's clients face. Approaching death with dignity and a sense of fulfilment has to be part of the difficult message that the fundraiser needs to convey.

The fundraising case should be based on the organisation's values and major achievements, as set out in the business plan. Selling the successes, emphasising who has been helped in the past and how it will ask for support from current and potential future donors, is vital.

There are four steps to building a case for support:

1. What is the organisation?
In the UK, it is a registered charity and company limited by guarantee. This has to be included in the case for support, both to comply with current legislation (in most countries) and because donors want and expect to see it when they are asked for money. It makes sense always to make clear that the organisation is a not-for-profit as this reassures donors, staff and beneficiaries.

2. What does it do?
The focus should be on succinctly describing the organisation's services, as well as emphasising how it delivers them cost effectively.

3. What does it want?
This sets out the particular projects (both current

and new) that require support. The full cost of each should be given in detail. How this will be packaged and presented depends on the type of funder or donor being approached.

4. Why should any donor support this cause?

This is the place to emphasise the emotional aspects of giving. Tell a brief and dramatic story of successes and the urgency of the appeal. This is sometimes called appealing to *hearts and minds*, as an effective case statement will be both emotionally powerful and factually accurate and inspiring.

These shopping lists are essential parts of a fundraising action plan…

Facts and figures are indispensable for this last element. If you ask someone to give you a hundred pounds, the response is quite likely to be, 'What for?' The case for support should answer this question before it is asked. The number of people that the organisation has helped (its outputs) and the difference it has made to their lives (its outcomes) will help to estimate what a unit of support could look like. Then it is possible to break project costs into easily visualised components. Such as:

• £10 will pay for initial advice to one more client.

• £100 will pay for 100 leaflets to explain the condition and its impact on those affected by it.

- £1,000 will pay for a small workshop to train volunteer visitors.

In this way the case will give donors a hook on which to hang their support, or a shopping list. The overall fundraising strategy should contain a range of plans for each project; the plans, in turn, should include details of project needs.

These shopping lists are essential parts of a fundraising action plan and a strategy should have such a list for most, if not all, the projects in the business plan.

… a case for support should belong to everyone…

There are also a few supplementary questions to answer and these should be defined too:

- How do we make a difference to people's lives?

- How do we continue to strive to be better than the competition?

- Do we make donations go a long way?

- Are we sensitive to those who use our services?

These apply to any nonprofit.

Involvement

To find the answers to these questions, Michael did some research into the results the Trust had achieved and feedback it had received from beneficiaries. He also looked into how other nonprofits in the field compared with the Trust and how effectively the Trust managed its resources.

To illustrate the wider impact of the Trust's work Michael was able to show how, for example, through early intervention patients can save themselves money and avoid putting additional pressure on the National Health Service (NHS). By teaching people to recognise the signs when their condition worsens and to take appropriate action, the Trust can prevent emergencies that would otherwise require a trip by ambulance to a hospital.

To be sure that he had sufficient information to make the case as powerful and potent as it could be, Michael showed Tony his ideas. They agreed that, as a case for support should belong to everyone, there should be a discussion about the document at the following week's staff meeting. Becoming a *listening* organisation appealed to Tony and he thought it would appeal to the board too. So he invited Michael to present his thoughts to the board at the next meeting, to get the trustees' views, as well as their agreement to and confirmation of the case for support.

So, the first thing Michael prepared to put in his fundraising suitcase was his reason for raising money for the Phoenix Trust, the case for support. But he had no time to daydream about the journey, for now he had quite a lot of people to see.

Learning points

1. Develop a compelling and appealing case for support.

2. Break project costs into easily visualised components – shopping lists for potential donors.

3. Project a positive image of your cause.

4. Ensure that all the communications tools describe and promote your organisation effectively to help you to raise as much money as they possibly can.

5. Make sure colleagues, board members and other key groups all have the opportunity to feel part of the newly defined case statement.

People

When you go on holiday or on a long trip, do you prefer to travel alone or with other people? If you're someone who likes to do things on your own, you may find fundraising isn't for you. Fundraising is a people business. It's no occupation for a dedicated loner. An ideal fundraising companion is likely to be someone with drive, enthusiasm and connections, good company, interesting and very good with people. But even though fundraisers often work on their own, they rarely succeed in isolation. In successful nonprofits, large and small, fundraising is everyone's business.

Valuable contributions

When Michael started preparing the Phoenix Trust's fundraising strategy he knew that he couldn't do it alone. He needed support – networks and contacts – if fundraising at the Trust was to be sustainable in the medium to long term. After all, one of his five principles is *to focus upon strategies for long-term thinking and income.*

Lots of different groups of people had valuable contributions to make in the creation and implementation of the strategy. Michael talked to a wide range of interested people. This included people with MJS and their families, volunteers, Tony, the finance staff – who set and monitor budgets – project delivery staff, the board, people running projects with the Trust, local health authority colleagues who work closely with the Trust, as well as possible future partners.

Michael wanted to ask everyone about different aspects of the Trust. Some of his questions were consistent for all, some were tailored for each group. He asked them about their views of the Trust's services, so that he could collect a portfolio of quotes to use in brochures, funding bids and when speaking publicly. He also listened attentively to views on what makes the Phoenix Trust unique, particularly effective and how it might improve.

Michael wanted help and support for his fundraising, so he asked everyone if they had ever done fundraising before – perhaps for other charities – and whether or not they would be able and willing to volunteer to help at events, or in other ways. Did they have friends or contacts who could help the Trust in any way? As he discussed the issues he continnously looked out for specific abilities, such as IT skills for setting up small databases, research skills, people who like public speaking, or who are natural organisers, and so on.

What he wanted from them was information…

His conversations with board members had a different slant, as he felt they might lead to new groups of potential supporters, such as members of the local golf club, or chamber of commerce. As MJS is specific to a minority of the general population, it was simple to focus upon what Michael saw as his primary target group for fundraising, those who live with the condition and their families. For example, he had recently spotted a photo of one of his board members in the local paper, smiling alongside a local hero – a tall football player who was pictured supporting another local cause. Michael knew that MJS had affected the footballer's daughter.

When he met staff, Michael made it clear that he didn't expect them to volunteer at his events, although they would be most welcome. What he wanted from them was information: about projects and their objectives, statistics that showed the great need for the services, details of the financial approach they were using. He needed this so that he could be confident that the costs he had looked at earlier were realistic and that nothing had been left out.

So by consulting widely, Michael put together, piece by piece, a picture of what people, inside and outside the Phoenix Trust community, thought about it. He also decided to ask if they could put a consultation activity – which would seek the views and suggestions of everyone involved with the Trust – into the charity's annual plan, as this would continue to inform so much of what they do.

Once this phase was complete, Michael could then create his strategy, confident that he had the necessary input from relevant people that would shape his approach and thinking.

Implementing the first principle

Next, Michael looked at funding methods and funders, to prepare a plan of how to deliver the strategy and finally to set up a reliable review process. His objective was not just to enable the Trust to raise enough money to fund its scheduled work, but even to generate a surplus that could be put into reserve. Here he was implementing his very first principle – to be the most learned fundraiser. He used the wealth of up-to-date fundraising information he had learned, or had access to, to create a strategy based upon expertise and excellent practice.

Spreading the workload

As soon he started formulating ideas for the outline of his strategy, Michael showed it to Tony and other colleagues, who discussed and refined it. Because Michael had worked so hard talking to people and researching the various documents there was little to change. Michael and Tony decided that once the strategy had been agreed and approved by the management and staff, Michael would get the chance to present it to the board for their discussion and ratification. Having this time is important because it gives fundraisers the chance to inspire trustees with their enthusiasm and competence and to galvanise the board's active participation in the plan too.

But once the strategy is agreed and approved, who will use it?

But once the strategy is agreed and approved, who will use it? Who will review its progress, and when? Michael is the only fundraiser at the Phoenix Trust, so he co-ordinates all fundraising activity and the amount that the Trust can put aside for investment in fundraising is not huge. This combination of limited time and money for investment dictates the mix of fundraising techniques Michael can choose from and the number of activities he can manage at one time. He has to make the most of his time by spreading the workload and getting others to support him.

It occurred to Michael that a new volunteer fundraising group, or committee, could be a great support, if made up of the right people with the right skills and background. He had to find people who already had experience and expertise in fundraising for healthcare not-for-profits, or who were familiar with the NHS funding arena, or who had an interest in the Trust and access to good networks of wealthy people. He thought that a board member, or two, would be useful, but they must be active and understand their specific fundraising role. He also thought it would be good to include someone with excellent organisation skills, to keep administrative functions ticking over.

It is important for the organisation's reputation that volunteer fundraisers are not left to their own devices.

One of Michael's tasks – his second principle – is to promote, by example, a culture of best practice in fundraising for the Trust, whether he is working with staff, the board, other volunteers, or his new committee. To do this he put together a concise fundraising information pack, which helps everyone to work with confidence.

More people… more money

From past experiences as a volunteer, Michael knows how important it is that volunteer fundraisers should receive appropriate support, help and guidance, both verbal and written. There are good reasons for this. They must ensure that their activities comply with the raft of legislation that applies to fundraising. This can cover such things as ways of asking for money to applying for licences or permits. It is important for the organisation's reputation that volunteer fundraisers are not left to their own devices. Supportive supervision will motivate volunteers and improve their chances of success.

Michael felt that, generally, the more people he could involve in the Trust's fundraising, the more money the Trust would raise. The fundraiser often manages the function and does some, but not all, of the work. For example, in his last post Michael had experience of undertaking the research, planning and preparation of funding applications and appeals, but he was usually expected to leave others to do the actual asking for money. Getting the right person to ask can make the difference between success and failure.

Any effective fundraising strategy has to be regularly reviewed and monitored and, at least annually, adjusted and updated in line with business plan developments. Michael set up a monitoring framework on his computer for monthly updates for himself and tied this in with his monthly support and supervision sessions with Tony. The Trust's fundraising progress is now easy for all to see.

As we've seen, Michael made a long list of all the people who will play a role in his strategy – people to consult, people to provide him with information, people to agree or assess his plan, people to help him to deliver, people to monitor and review – all people with different points of view. He has indeed confirmed that fundraising truly is a people business.

Learning points

1. **Never forget that fundraising is primarily about people – networks and contacts.**

2. **Use your trustees and other volunteers to assist your fundraising in any way that is appropriate.**

3. **Consider setting up a fundraising group or committee. But make sure that you fill it with the right people.**

4. **Prepare a simple but eloquent fundraising activity information pack, which will help and guide volunteers who assist with the fundraising. Enable them to adopt best practice in fundraising in all they undertake.**

5. **Set up frameworks for regular strategy review and monitoring.**

Building the strategy on firm foundations

We have seen already how a carefully planned journey can remove the uncertainty about arriving in an unfamiliar place. By mapping out your itinerary and making choices about how to spend your time, you can have a fair idea of what to expect. Then you can pack your suitcase, collect your holiday currency and get ready for an adventure – or a rest.

Excitement or difficulty

Even though planning every step of the way means
that you are prepared, no one can say that the
unexpected won't happen, it always does.
Sometimes the unknown becomes an exciting
opportunity; at other times it can give rise to
inconvenience, or difficulty. It is all
part of the fun of the journey.
Still, having an overall plan
will almost always help.

He couldn't afford to fail.

Fundraising is no different. In
order to fundraise successfully
so that all the projects in the Phoenix Trust
business plan could go ahead, Michael had a lot of
work to do. And he couldn't afford to fail. If he did,
then the Trust's clients – the people who benefit
from its services – would lose out on the services
they need. That's why any fundraiser in Michael's
position has to start by putting a fundraising
strategy in place.

Michael and Tony had already discussed how a
typical fundraising strategy document would cover
at least a seven-year time frame. The past three
years provide the funding history, the current year
shows up-to-the-minute practice and the remainder
of the strategy is the planning for the next three
years, possibly longer.

To set out the framework for the strategy and just
what information to include in it, Michael drew up
a list of headings to make sure he left nothing out.

The first section of his strategy is titled:

Part 1
Legal status and governance structure

To begin with Michael set the scene for fundraising, without repeating too much of the detail in the business plan. The legal status and governance structure of a charity are relevant because this knowledge will give any donor confidence in the organisation's overall legitimacy.

The Phoenix Trust is a legally established nonprofit (in this case registered with the Charity Commission the UK's regulatory body for nonprofit organisations), and a company limited by guarantee (registered in the UK with Companies House). Its annual report and accounts are submitted to the Charity Commission every year. The Trust is governed by a board of trustees, there are several board committees and soon there will be a fundraising committee.

Next, Michael considered where the Trust is positioned in the nonprofit sector in general. It is a national charity, albeit a small one, and this will attract funders who choose to support countrywide initiatives. At the same time, it doesn't have the resources to deliver services in all regions of the country.

He gave his next section the heading:

Part 2
A background to our organisation, including its position in the nonprofit sector, local influences and legislation. Include an analysis of the external environment and how this influences fundraising.

The 'national but small' ingredients are worth thinking about in planning the strategy. As fundraiser for a health-related nonprofit, Michael keeps up to date not only with general legislation about fundraising, but also with best practice guidelines and funding opportunities in the related health fields. He relies upon Tony and the Trust's professional staff for this knowledge. Of course he also needs to keep up to date with the local funding situation, as this will provide invaluable information about his opportunities for raising money from local sources.

When planning for success it is essential that fundraisers know what is going on outside their own organisations. This includes an appreciation of other nonprofits and agencies doing similar work. Are relationships with them good or bad – is there collaboration, or criticism? What is the potential for growth, are there any constraints on activities, are there any threats to the work and the way the organisation delivers it? Is there evidence of peaks and troughs in the local, national, or international economy that could affect the nonprofit. All of these could influence the kinds of fundraising an organisation might take up, and in what timescale.

Michael and Tony together prepared an analysis of

all the potential external influences, both positive and negative, on the Trust and shared it widely. This exercise gave Michael an understanding of how the Phoenix Trust interacted with other organisations. He relied upon Tony to look at the potential for alliances, for threats, for collaboration and for partnerships in service delivery. He would do the same for fundraising.

Michael's strategy outline was built on firm foundations. He was ready to look at the values that underpinned the Phoenix Trust.

... there was an excellent response to the dramatic stories the Trust tells.

Part 3
Vision, mission, core values and beliefs

Tony had already confirmed that these had been agreed by the board and were succinctly described in the business plan. Michael also wanted to focus on these values in his strategy. After all, what would motivate donors to choose to support the Trust? What would make the work of the Trust appeal to a wide range of individuals? As we know, when he started to prepare the case for support he had interviewed staff and beneficiaries and learned that there was an excellent response to the emotive and dramatic stories the Trust tells. Communicating these stories and the impact the Trust has on the lives of people with MJS made the difference and generated interest in giving it support. Again, he was listening. He decided that what appeals to existing donors is the ethos of the Trust.

The Trust's *vision, mission,* and *core values* are:

Vision – dream scenario
A world where MJS no longer exists.

Mission – overall reason for existing – what we do
The Phoenix Trust exists to educate individuals with MJS and their families about the syndrome so that they are able to live happy, productive lives; as well as helping at times of crisis. The Trust supports them in working with specialist healthcare professionals to adopt strategies for the short, medium and longer term, regardless of the severity of the condition.

Core values – what we believe in
The Trust values the rights of each individual and respects their choices.

The next step is:

Part 4
Our major achievements and analysis of strengths, weaknesses, opportunities and threats (SWOT analysis)

Michael found a list of the Phoenix Trust's major achievements, which had been prepared by the board and senior staff and would be great to use for fundraising. He also discovered the SWOT analysis that the board had completed.

Michael was pleased to see this analysis. It showed that his colleagues and the board were aware of the weaknesses he had identified, such as the absence of effective communications, the lack of a strong identity or brand, and the over-dependence upon a few areas of funding. Although these were listed as weaknesses, Michael felt that now he was in post he could turn them into strengths, by making sure that he always has communications that are as good as they possibly can be. He felt that it was important to include the parts of the SWOT analysis that were pertinent to fundraising in his strategy.

Michael's next stage focused on communication:

Part 5
Who we are and why we deserve your support

Here Michael set out the case for support, which we examined earlier. Michael felt that a robust, well-presented case for support would be the bedrock of his fundraising. He also wanted to say something about the Trust's brand, fully aware that this was an area ripe for development. Brand is defined as,

Not as how you want people to view your organisation and its work, but rather the set of ideas, images, feelings, beliefs and values that are carried around in a person's head.

Michael felt that this is a good definition for the Trust, one that would be very useful when its brand was reviewed and redefined, which he regarded as an urgent task.

It was clear to Michael that a successful and

targeted approach to communications would be essential for his fundraising. In fact communications and fundraising are impossible to separate. After all, if we fundraisers listen with care to our donors, give them choices and make sure that we offer them what they are looking for, we are promoting our organisations and making it easy for donors to support us.

Now that Michael had laid down the foundations for the strategy, it was time to consider a number of funding issues. How to go about generating the income required by the Trust to meet the financial objectives of the business plan? And what could be done to plan for a longer, more robust financial future, with long-term sustainability in mind? He would have to be careful and balance short-term survival with the strategies he wanted to focus upon, which would yield longer-term stability. Once again he was reminded of those five cornerstones of his personal approach.

He summarised this task as the next step in his plan:

Part 6
Identify the current funding situation. Look at income for the current year and the past three years, including income from all sources

Michael's initial examination of the Trust's income and expenditure had given him a good understanding of the general financial picture. Then he had narrowed down his investigation and focused upon income, as this is most important for fundraising. By looking at the income over the past three years by type, he had seen that it had almost always come from statutory sources – from a range of local government, local health authority and government health-based programmes. He knew that government funding was based upon priorities, and priorities were likely to change over time. And although the funds didn't seem to be disappearing from these sources yet, he was sure that relying heavily upon one source of funds was unwise. He had heard many tales, in his last post, about fundraising failing due to over-reliance upon one area of funding.

Michael's plan was to work towards spreading the income beyond statutory sources. Although his previous fundraising experience had been with foundations and trusts, he knew that the best asset any charity can own is a healthy and growing database of individual donors. All the evidence shows that, when properly nurtured and developed, a solid, substantial donor base provides the most reliable funding over the long term, particularly if regular (monthly) committed giving and legacy (bequest) giving can be developed. Now that Michael was working as the Trust's dedicated fundraiser, he would have the opportunity to explore additional ways to fund services that, he believed, would enable the Trust to survive and thrive.

Learning points

1. Set out a framework for the strategy. Draw up a list of headings, so that nothing is left out.

2. Prepare a detailed analysis of the external environment for your organisation, including all relevant social, technological, economic, environmental, political, legal and ethical external indicators. This is known as a **STEEPLE** analysis.

3. Be clear about the vision, mission, core values and beliefs of your organisation.

4. Decide what will appeal to your donors.

5. Find out your organisation's achievements, then look at its strengths, weaknesses, opportunities and threats.

6. Focus on communication.

7. Develop your organisation's brand.

8. Look for any additional fundraising opportunities.

Making the most of opportunities

In its fundraising journey, the Phoenix Trust was now getting into really interesting new territory as Michael began to expand the details of his fundraising strategy.

Once Michael had set out his analysis of the Trust's past fundraising performance, his next step was to take a considered look at what was possible in fundraising and to start researching future options for the Phoenix Trust. Clearly he wanted to apply the very best and most up-to-date fundraising theory and practice.

Part 7
Put together a plan that matches business plan objectives and budgets with fundraising opportunities

As we have seen Michael had studied the Trust's business plan closely and had been relieved to see that it set out the strategic aims as well as the operational objectives of the organisation (see first chapter).

Now it was time to match the funding needs detailed in the business plan with fundraising opportunities. Michael had to take a considered look at what was possible and to start researching future options for the Trust. This part of the work never seems to get finished, as opportunities and changes in fundraising are continuous.

Part 8
Undertake a comprehensive analysis of all potential funding and fundraising tools

Michael had to plan for the short term (the next year), the medium term (two or perhaps three years) and the longer term (more than three years). He also planned for excellence and sustainability – as in his principles – and he was determined that the Trust should build a reserve for the future and for emergencies.

As sole fundraiser at the Trust, Michael needed to improve his skills, so he started by signing up to a masterclass that was taking place locally. He also thought it would be worthwhile to invest a little of his limited budget in some really good books on various aspects of fundraising. He also gathered together a lot of valuable information from fundraising websites all over the world.

He arranged an informal gathering of his peers in the health field, which was extremely useful. One fundraiser told him about different schemes that offered packages, including loans, investment and grants to nonprofits. Another was raising money by renting out office space in the organisation's building. He also told Michael about a community foundation that owned a cemetery and earned money from this! Obviously, it would be a good idea to continue to meet informally with other fundraisers who faced similar issues.

As his research continued, he drew up a list of other opportunities available to the Trust.

... he became convinced that individual donations would be the long-term solution...

Donations from individuals

The more Michael thought about it, the more he became convinced that individual donations would be the long-term solution to the need for regular, unrestricted income, i.e. donations that can be used for any purpose at all. He had a few ideas on how to achieve these, which included:

• A low-cost mailing to existing volunteers that would be produced, tested and mailed in house.

• Information evenings with a 'how you can help'

table as a gentle reminder that the charity needs money.

• He would write a regular column in the bright, redesigned newsletter that would explain how donations, or gifts in wills, make a difference.

• There would be a fundraising element on the Trust's planned website.

• He decided to test using the telephone to talk to donors, for instance to say thank you for an unexpected generous gift, or to discuss setting up a regular donation.

• Trying out a public collection using volunteer collectors.

• In the medium term he would look into the best ways to use electronic media for low-cost fundraising, including creating donation links from the website, maximising the use of emails and text messaging.

Whatever he chose, Michael knew that, like most fundraising organisations, the Trust would benefit from starting a donor-focused style of relationship building that would underpin all their initiatives to attract individual donors.

Tax recovery
In the UK, the government is encouraging the growth of voluntary giving by providing tax incentives for charitable donations from individuals. For this to succeed at the Phoenix Trust, the whole organisation, not just Michael, has to work as a team.

Contracts for delivering public services

Contracts for the delivery of public services are becoming more common in the nonprofit sector.

However, preparing to deliver public services takes a lot of time and planning. This income is unlikely to revolutionise fundraising overnight but it is still worth investigating. If contracts are delivered effectively and also generate a surplus then the nonprofit can be free to use the extra income to undertake some pilot projects, or test some more creative, even risky, trial initiatives.

But – and it's a fairly large but – they should be viewed with caution.

But – and it's a fairly large but – they should be viewed with caution. In the UK, when preparing a budget most commercial organisations make provisions for overheads, such as staff holidays or sickness, unexpected price increases, economic downturns, etc. At the moment few voluntary organisations do this, consequently they are often very much cheaper and win the contract. But if they haven't budgeted correctly, this can result in a shortfall and there may be inadequate funds to cover all costs.

Also, the current culture of contracts is based upon the commissioning of services that stipulate the details of the service from the point of view of the commissioning body – usually a local government authority. This often leaves no room for service development or creative problem solving.

Trading

For an organisation such as the Phoenix Trust, trading could be within the primary purpose of the charity, such as service development consultancy to local or regional authorities. It could even be on an international basis, particularly to countries with a greater incidence of MJS. It could be non-primary purpose trading, for instance the Trust could buy a building larger than its needs and rent out surplus space as a way to generate unrestricted income.

Trading also covers charity, or goodwill, shops, sale of Christmas cards and gifts, maybe even a year-round catalogue, or through the organisation's website, which could include items featuring the charity's logo. However, a small organisation such as the Phoenix Trust has to consider whether results from such activities merit the investment they take, both financial and time.

Foundations and trusts

Grants from foundations and trusts can be very useful for any short- or middle-term requirements. For example, just after Michael joined the Trust, there had been a lot of interest in the media around an unusual pilot project for a medical condition similar to MJS, which had produced some great results. Ever since, patients with MJS had been clamouring for the Phoenix Trust to set up a similar scheme; however, as yet no funds were available and there was little likelihood of any statutory funding. The project was included in the overall business plan, but there was no income strand in place for it. This is the sort of project that is often of interest to charitable foundations and trusts.

From his experience in his previous job, Michael knew that anyone approaching a foundation should be sure how long the project will need funding. If you are looking for funds for, say, five years, make sure that you apply to foundations prepared to make long-term grants. Many give them for just one year, which can create uncertainty within the charity. If you do decide to go ahead with an application, and it is granted, make sure that you have a plan (an exit strategy) in place for how you are going to continue the project when that grant comes to an end. You don't want to be in the position of having to cut the service, or make staff redundant.

Exit strategies apply to all grants, whatever their duration.

Exit strategies apply to all grants, whatever their duration. All funders whose grants are coming to an end should be given a comprehensive and appropriate final report and assessment document. Grant recipients have to be sure that if they approach these donors in future they will be remembered as a competent and successful grantee.

Government grants

Although a useful source of funds, these grants, like contracts, can be fraught with danger if the budget isn't carefully prepared. It is essential to make sure that they are not merely a route to raising new funds and are, in fact, a means to delivering your organisation's objectives. Government grants cannot be relied upon for the long term, so it is vital to plan an exit strategy to cover the gap in income after the grant comes to an end

Events

These are often a good way to raise a nonprofit's profile, either locally or nationally. In the case of the Phoenix Trust, Michael had already identified someone who might consider helping to put together a guest list – remember the football player earlier on? However, events are often costly to run and time consuming. They can also be very risky, unless there is a guaranteed guest list filled with individuals with the desire and potential to make large donations. There also has to be an influential network of willing ticket sellers to ensure that every table is filled. Any charity working in an area of significant economic deprivation should be careful not to give offence by holding a glitzy and costly event.

Corporate fundraising

Companies often support nonprofits largely as a means of getting good publicity for themselves and are interested in what the nonprofit can offer them. Michael could not compete with large organisations that had budgets for working with national companies, but he felt that the Trust could be of interest to local businesses, for instance those who supplied goods, or services to the Trust. Also, he was confident that employees of local companies who had a family member, or a friend, with MJS would be prepared to ask their employer to join in a partnership with the Trust. There are many workshops, books and websites that help fundraisers prepare an approach to commercial organisations.

Michael now had a comprehensive list of new fundraising tools to explore and choose from, but he was sure that to provide continuous funding of all projects it is essential to have a high percentage of unrestricted funds. He investigated how to achieve this extremely carefully before making any recommendations to

... it is essential to have a high percentage of unrestricted funds.

the board. Some trustees were concerned at the associated costs of fundraising, especially about testing some of the new initiatives suggested in his strategy. The board was new to this and had only just approved the allocation of salary costs to fundraising. Given their almost inevitable caution, even scepticism, Michael would have to be cautious too and rigorous in his analysis, in order to convince them to invest in fundraising. For example, to take advantage of legacy fundraising or a direct mail programme for donations from individuals, some upfront expenditure would be required.

Next he reviewed what the Trust had to do internally to enable fundraising to really succeed.

Part 9
Identify the additional internal resources required to implement the fundraising strategy

Before any new strategy is implemented, it is important to review the organisation as a whole. Michael and Tony wanted to integrate fundraising into the heart of the Trust, so it was important to prepare the entire organisation for more active fundraising. Michael had already spent a lot of time talking to people about the strategy and fundraising in general, to get the rest of the staff and the board more involved. Now was the time to reinforce the message that, in successful nonprofits, fundraising success is everyone's business.

Michael and Tony, together with members of the financial team, reviewed the finance systems to establish if they could accommodate increased fundraising activity and a marked rise in volume and type of donations. This highlighted that extra staff would be needed to administer the potential additional fundraising and, although it wasn't yet time to buy a dedicated fundraising database, it would almost certainly be necessary a few months later so provision was required in the budget.

Michael's plans were ambitious, but there was only a modest budget at this early stage. However, he was confident that in subsequent years he would contribute to the planning stages of the budget-setting process.

Michael's strategy outline was falling into place and

it was time to put some quality controls in place, to ensure he was fundraising effectively.

So the final part of his strategy was about monitoring and evaluating progress.

He would not be afraid of bad news stories either....

Part 10
Introduce and implement monitoring systems to check progress and evaluation systems to inform future planning

Before deciding where to allocate the Trust's scarce resources, Michael wanted to carry out fundraising trials or small-scale pilots. He intended to have an internal monitoring system that could be used alongside the business plan to keep track of how different fundraising techniques compared, and how useful each one proved to be for the Trust.

He also planned to put regular monitoring dates into his activities and to collect data in his work as a matter of course. He wanted to instil an approach where collecting and using data was standard practice. He would collect stories from projects and encourage everyone to contribute to the assembling of good news tales to use for fundraising and publicity. He would not be afraid of bad news stories either, as these can be very informative for learning and can sometimes generate happy endings if handled appropriately.

Finally, at the end of each fundraising appeal or campaign, he would be sure to prepare a full evaluation of the process and its results for the Trust to use for future plans. So monitoring goes beyond financial monitoring, to monitoring what aspects of each fundraising activity are working well, where there are difficulties, why these are arising and how to find solutions early on.

Now with all elements in place, Michael is nearing the end of the strategy planning. He just needs to frame his conclusion, and make the final step.

He had discovered some areas as yet unexplored at the Trust...

Part 11
Conclusion

The final part of Michael's strategy involves identifying any issues outstanding for him, as well as tying together its overall objectives.

He had discovered some areas as yet unexplored at the Trust, such as an annual risk assessment review, a communications strategy owned by everyone and the dissemination and use of information on trends in the treatment of MJS across the world.

These are just a few of the big issues that Michael will learn from, which will be important for him and will be part of the general maturing of the Trust. As the Trust's first fundraiser, his task is daunting, but he was encouraged by the attitude Tony, the staff and the board have towards him and his plans.

Michael is clear about his overall objectives. Personally he is determined to adhere to the five cornerstones of his personal goals and as far as his work aim is concerned, that is simple, in his words it is,

'To ensure that the Phoenix Trust receives sufficient income for the short, medium and longer term so that our services will be available and tailored to anyone who might benefit from them; and that we have sufficient reserves for exploration of new approaches for supporting people living with MJS.'

Michael's new strategy will be accompanied by an action plan, and the way these two documents are used will make all the difference to the success of fundraising at the Trust.

Learning points

1. Prepare a detailed analysis of all available means of fundraising so that gaps and opportunities can be identified and their potential can be tested.

2. Make a rigorous case for appropriate investment in fundraising. Encourage trustees and others to view expenditure that will lead to a return as an investment, not merely a cost.

3. Identify the additional internal resources required to implement the fundraising strategy.

4. Regularly and carefully monitor performance so that decisions can be guided by tangible results.

5. Define the aim of your fundraising in a simple sentence that everyone can rally around.

The fundraising action plan

The journey is planned, the flight's booked, your case is packed and you are ready for departure. Now it's time to go, to have the adventure.

Michael's next step was to create a fundraising action plan, which is simply a summary of who does what and when to implement the detail of the strategy.

The fundraising strategy shows how funds can be raised to meet the business plan objectives over a three-year period, specifying the short, medium and long-term fundraising objectives. For the action plan, Michael needed to calculate, estimate, or at least make an educated guess as to what fundraising would be happening in each quarter of the coming year, and who would be doing it.

The fundraising action plan is a tool for doing

Getting things done

The fundraising action plan is a tool for doing. To make it manageable it is split into years and then into three-month segments, or quarters. Michael asked a few, more experienced, friends to show him their own action plans. He used their structure, approach and style in the preparation of his own plan. At the end of the first year he would review the fundraising programme, using what actually happened to develop the plan for the following two years. He created a *rolling* plan to accommodate developments as he progressed.

The action plan is based upon SMART objectives. SMART is a simple model where:

S = specific, M = measurable, A = achievable, R = realistic and T = time-bound.

All components of the plan are measured against these five criteria.

However, opinions vary slightly on the definition. For instance,

S = specific, significant, stretching.

M = measurable, meaningful, motivational.

A = achievable, agreed upon, acceptable, action-oriented.

R = realistic, relevant, reasonable, reward, results-oriented.

T = time-based, timely, tangible, trackable.

Each organisation has to decide which is the most appropriate for its needs.

Michael recorded, measured and analysed the risks of each initiative in a fundraising risk register. He then compared the risks against the benefits. Once he had completed several of these risk comparisons, he asked for Tony's views, reactions from other senior colleagues and the input of the board's fundraising committee so that they could decide whether or not the benefits outweighed the risks.

Because the action plan is derived from the fundraising strategy, which in turn is derived from the business plan, the structure, referencing and numbering of all documents are linked. Michael's fundraising action plan was a list of SMART objectives and under these he listed the actions, who would do the work, who else was involved (even in a minor role), who would supervise completion of the tasks and give support with problem solving, and the timescale for completion. Michael produced a dummy version (see next page) for the first quarter and tried it out on some of his colleagues for their feedback and input.

Sample of a fundraising action plan 2009–2010

Derived from Phoenix Trust business plan 2009–2011 and the fundraising strategy

AIM	OBJECTIVE	ACTION
Aim 3 To raise the sum required for costs of satellite office, 2009-11, roughly estimated at £20K per annum (Michael).	**Objective 3.1** By 30 June 2009 to have a detailed and costed fundraising plan to achieve aim 3 (Michael). **Objective 3.2** By 30 July 2009 to have completed investigation of potential funding mix for premises costs (Michael).	**Action 3.1.1** By 1 May 2009 to have agreed costings for office rent and other expenditure with finance and budget holder (Michael and Fiona). **Action 3.1.2** By 31 May to have completed case for support for aim 3 (Michael). **Action 3.1.3** By 30 June to have project detail and budget approved by line manager (Michael and Tony). **Action 3.1.4** By 1 September to have made a list of likely foundations to approach along with timetable and priority rating (Michael).

Understanding and agreement

Communication of the importance of the fundraising strategy to staff, the board, volunteers and, in certain cases, the beneficiaries is a major strand of the fundraising action plan. Without understanding and agreement from everyone, plus a willingness to support the strategy, there is a real danger of spending time, energy and precious funds on writing a comprehensive fundraising strategy, only for it to sit in the fundraising office, pristine and unopened. Because Michael had included a range of staff and other stakeholders in his original consultation, its content wasn't new or unfamiliar to them. He had made it clear that input from project delivery staff would be essential for effective fundraising and, once they understood why their views would be needed, they expressed a willingness to help.

Each organisation has to decide which is the most appropriate for its needs.

To be sure of reaching and involving everyone, Michael held an information session during a lunchtime, offering sandwiches, cake and coffee to all who came along. He held this event on a day when the board was meeting so that he secured maximum attendance. As a back up, he gave out a question and answer leaflet, which summarised the session by giving the overall aims of the strategy, its structure and how it linked to the business plan objectives. He also sent this to people who hadn't been able to attend.

Michael knew that his strategy and plan were taking the board of the Phoenix Trust into some unknown and potentially scary territory. After all, before he had been employed, fundraising at the Phoenix Trust had been haphazard. There had been little appreciation at board level that fundraising would require investment or expenditure. Since then the board's collective understanding of the issues had come a long way, thanks to careful preparation and good briefing from the senior management team, together with clear explanation and regular updating. Now, Michael felt that, individually and collectively, the board was ready to accept enthusiastically all the implications of the changes that needed to be made. He was confident that they would give their full backing to the strategy and plan he was about to put before them.

Information for funders

Communication with funders should be a priority for all nonprofits. Rather than send the full strategy, Michael produced an executive summary to send to funders, along with the tailored case for support. He thought that funders and other outside bodies would find the existence of the fundraising strategy a useful tool, one that would reinforce the Trust's commitment to transparency and accountability to donors.

He also created a template to ensure that all details of a funder's interaction with, and from, the Trust were recorded. It specified:

- Date of notification from funder.

- Date thank you sent.

- Names provided to funder for future liaison.

- Monitoring dates and requirements. These are the dates specified by funders when they expect a report on the progress of the project or funding cycle. It is the responsibility of the nonprofit to get the reports to the funder on time if they want the next part of the money.

- Progress reports sent.

- Annual report sent.

- Invitation to event.

- Invitation for face-to-face progress meeting.

- Other specific/relevant information. It is important that whoever is using the template can amend it to include any additional details that an individual funder might have requested. Or even to include some information that has not been asked for, but that the fundraiser thinks might be interesting to the funder.

Learning points

1. The fundraising strategy involves everyone. So plan ways to present it that will be accessible to all. Have a written summary for those who can't be enthused personally.

2. Make sure the strategy is accompanied by a time-specific fundraising action plan.

3. Use SMART objectives – specific, measurable, achievable, realistic, time-bound – for the action plan.

4. Plan to present a summary of the strategy to key external audiences too.

5. Prepare a template that records all a funder's details, including dates when they have requested reports and when they were sent.

Journey's end – and a new beginning

The traveller is back at home, journey complete, rested, invigorated and daydreaming about the next trip. But first, you decide to write up the adventure so you can look back and remember it and, crucially, be sure to save all the lessons you have learned to use for the next journey.

It is now 12 months since Michael joined the Phoenix Trust and it has been a hectic, but stimulating, year for everyone, thanks in large part to the employment of their first fundraiser.

Michael's achievements have been impressive. He's created a generic fundraising case for support. His fundraising strategy has been enthusiastically accepted by everyone involved with the Trust. He has begun to make headway against each of the main objectives that his strategy describes. There is little opposition to supplying him with project budgets, or barriers to his attempts at describing projects in jargon-free language.

His fundraising strategy has been enthusiastically accepted by everyone involved with the Trust.

Year one has been successful for Michael, not just because of the fundraising results but also in the way that the strategic approach he championed appears to be becoming embedded in the culture of the Phoenix Trust. Tony was delighted to be told that his supportive style of overseeing Michael and positive attitude to fundraising had really helped.

Michael has successfully developed his career, particularly through undertaking training designed to help him to introduce and test a few new techniques. He has concluded a very successful negotiation with a number of existing funders – persuading them to extend funding from single to multiple year agreements. And he has chalked up some early successes in fundraising from individuals. The strategy for year one has been now confirmed as reasonably accurate and achievable. But some problems have been identified too.

Nice problem... and not so nice

The first of these is rather a nice problem to have. As Michael had anticipated, the Trust now urgently needs to invest in a dedicated fundraising database. Record keeping is becoming a problem due to the significant growth in income and increased volume of donations from a number of sources.

Strategic plans are not static but evolve constantly.

Michael knows from discussion with fellow fundraisers that the second problem might prove more difficult to overcome. He wants to develop the Trust's board fundraising committee into more than a supportive opinion-giving body. It has to be an exemplary fundraiser in its own right, with a few prestigious names associated with it. He intends to pilot an exclusive event targeted only at those with the potential to make substantial gifts. Quite a challenge, as changing the culture of fundraising committees is often a frustrating experience. But it can be done – as many successful fundraising organisations have proved.

Evolution

Strategic plans are not static but evolve constantly. Michael already has a few new additions he wants to make to the second year of his strategy. The first thing to consider is a budget for the fundraising department, e.g. when the Trust starts using a wider range of funding techniques, Michael will need administrative support staff. He will have to calculate when they will be needed and what the costs will be.

Communications at the Phoenix Trust are much improved. The annual report and accounts have been redesigned to be more interesting and appealing and a short summary leaflet promoting the Trust has been printed. However, the budget for the next year's communications will have to be much higher if they are to be of a good enough standard to reflect the Trust's new fundraising professionalism.

This activity hadn't gone as planned.

During the first year, Michael had tried to explore the Trust's earning potential from joint activities, contracts and particularly from catalogue and on-line trading. He had even found a volunteer to undertake the necessary desk research to find out what other similar organisations were doing. This activity hadn't gone as planned because Michael's lack of time had prevented him from giving adequate support to his volunteer. Now it will be a higher priority, which will be reflected in the next year's action plan and budget.

Continuous change

Michael feels that commissioned work and procurement could be helpful for the Trust to access additional contracted work. There are also possibilities for loan income, selling expertise, or acting as a consultant on MJS to other health authorities. Some of this is his role to tackle, but a time-limited task group might address other aspects more successfully.

He has also been looking at how services were progressing to see if there were examples of excellance that could enhance fundraising for the Trust. For instance, the week after Tony had given a presentation at a regional health conference about an innovative project the Trust had undertaken, a large donation had been received, which the donor said had been inspired by Tony's presentation. Obviously, Michael is going to make sure that this – and any others in the future – will receive maximum publicity.

It will be reviewed, revised and updated at the end of each year…

It would seem that a strategy is never complete. It will be reviewed, revised and updated at the end of each year, because of inevitable, if not always anticipated, events and consequent adjustments to the overall business plan.

The senior team at the Phoenix Trust has started thinking about a planning weekend, which will take place in the middle of year three to review the end of the existing business plan and put in place the bare bones of the next one. Michael is already considering the fundraising action plan that will accompany it.

The start of another journey.

Learning points

1. Develop your board fundraising committee so that it is an exemplary fundraiser in its own right. If you don't have a board fundraising committee – start one.

2. Start a budget-setting process.

3. Make sure that fundraising communications are of a sufficiently high standard.

4. Build on successes.

5. Be prepared to constantly review, revise and update the strategy and action plan.

Glossary

Annual report and accounts
In the UK, charites whose gross income exceeds £25,000 must file accounts and the trustees' annual report with the Charity Commission annually. Charites whose gross income exceeds £10,000 must send a completed annual return to the Charity Commision

Bequest income or legacy income
Money, goods or property left in a will to an individual or nonprofit. Legacies are deducted from the value of an estate before inheritance tax is calculated.

Board fundraising committee
The committee of a board of trustees that has overall responsibility for fundraising. Sometimes they actively fundraise.

Board members, or trustees, or members of board of directors, or management committee members
Members of the governing body of a nonprofit.

Business plan
The strategic plan for three to five years that maps out the range of work to be undertaken and how it will be carried out. The annual version of this plan is called the operational plan or annual plan.

Charity, not-for-profit, or nonprofit
An organisation that exists to meet a defined need and reinvests any surplus or profit into the organisation.

Commissioned services
Public services that may be delivered by a private company or a nonprofit as well as by a public authority. The process of selection is called tendering or bidding.

Committed or regular giving
Gifts of money to a nonprofit that are made direct from a donor's bank account on a regular basis.

Communications strategy
A plan that maps out the nonprofit's approach to how it tells everyone about its work and why it deserves support. This strategy co-ordinates with the nonprofit's other strategic documents – the business plan and the fundraising strategy.

Company limited by guarantee
In the UK, a charitable organisation that is registered as a company but does not have shares. Any surplus is reinvested in the company. Trustees are called directors.

Core costs
Also called overhead costs and include running costs such as rent, heating and insurance. These may be divided between projects in order to accurately cost a nonprofit's services.

Corporate fundraising
Raising money from businesses.

Database
A record-keeping system of a list of names, addresses and personal details that a nonprofit collects and uses in various ways. Typically, if the list is more than a hundred names this information is managed most efficiently as computer records. It is an essential tool for fundraising.

Direct mail appeals
A programme of focused postal or email fundraising appeals sent to names held on your database. These can be low-cost internally prepared mailings or huge and professionally produced communications.

Donor development
Entering into a relationship with donors that encourages them to increase their commitment and giving to a nonprofit.

Earned income
Income that is the result of trading that may or may not be related to an organisation's central purpose. Selling a sweatshirt with a logo on it is earned income that actively promotes organisational aims. Renting out rooms in a building for public use is not charitable, but can generate useful income for the nonprofit to use.

Fundraising information pack
A pack of information designed by fundraisers to assist volunteers in fundraising on behalf of a nonprofit. It will include information about how to fundraise and also give guidance on how to handle money and any other legal or best practice requirements.

Governance
The behaviour of the board and how it adheres to the rules set down for how a nonprofit should be run.

Legal status
How the laws of a country recognise the nonprofit organisation.

Legislation
The framework of laws that regulate how a nonprofit must behave. These change over time and will differ from one country to another.

Listening organisation
A nonprofit that is focused upon learning from what it hears from its stakeholders.

Logo
The unique emblem or design that is used to distinguish a specific nonprofit's brand.

National Health Service (NHS)
The health service in the UK.

Operational plan/objectives
The short-term plans that are measured on a regular basis.

Outcomes
Results of a project that are long lasting but may be difficult to assess, such as the benefits of counselling.

Outputs
Short-term results that are easy to measure, for instance numbers of children attending a breakfast

club before school, or people having a medical check-up from a mobile health clinic.

Project
A discrete piece of work or initiative that has its own budget and resources allocated to it, such as staff, accommodation and facilities.

Public collection
An appeal for funds that takes place in a public place. It could be a collection of envelopes on a door-to-door basis, or using collecting tins, or covered buckets in a shopping mall or at a parade.

Registered charity
A nonprofit in the UK that is registered with the Charity Commission.

Reserves
Surplus funds that the nonprofit puts aside for future use. Reserves may be invested.

Restricted income
Grant or donation income given to fund a specific project or piece of work that cannot be used for anything else.

Rolling plan
An ongoing plan that continues for several years and uses learning from early years to inform later ones.

Strapline
A short phrase that helps explain a logo or nonprofit's name. For example, March of Dimes – *the leading nonprofit organisation for pregnancy and baby health.* The strapline is in italics.

Trusts and foundations

Private grant-making organisations, often the product of family or corporate wealth, that exist to give funds to other nonprofits. They offer the founder a way to use his or her money for good causes 'in perpetuity', as well as to lower the tax bill.

Volunteers

People who undertake work for a nonprofit out of choice and who do not receive a salary for their work. They may receive expenses.

About the 'Tiny Essentials' series

The book you hold in your hands is part of a series of little books with a big mission. They focus on what really matters in one key area of voluntary sector management. Each book's purpose is to provide the essentials of its subject in an entertaining, easily digestible form, so people who otherwise wouldn't dream of reading a business book can effortlessly and enjoyably get access to what they really need to know.

Books in the 'Tiny Essentials' series are delightfully free of padding, waffle and over-blown theories. Extraneous material has been reduced to a minimum. Each book so lives up to its title that there's just no room for anything other than the essence of what really matters in the subject area, and how to order your priorities.

This 'Tiny' focuses on what every fundraiser, CEO and board member needs to know about preparing and implementing a fundraising strategy. Other books in the 'Tiny' series are:

Tiny Essentials of Fundraising, by Neil Sloggie

Tiny Essentials of Writing for Fundraising, by George Smith

Tiny Essentials of Major Gift Fundraising, by Neil Sloggie

Tiny Essentials of an Effective Volunteer Board, by Ken Burnett

Tiny Essentials of Raising Money from Foundations and Trusts, by Jo Habib

Tiny Essentials of Monthly Committed Giving, by Harvey McKinnon

To be published in 2009:

Tiny Essentials of Donor Loyalty, by Professor Adrian Sargeant

Tiny Essentials of Donor Care, by Jonathon Grapsas

All can be ordered at www.whitelionpress.com

A promise from The White Lion Press

Enjoy the best books on fundraising and voluntary sector development. Books by The White Lion Press will repay your investment many times over – and you'll enjoy reading them too. But if your purchase is damaged in any way, or if you feel any of our products do not live up to your expectations simply return them to us and we will issue you with a full refund, including any reasonable associated costs. We'll ask you to tell us why, so we can put right anything that might be wrong, but we won't quibble. Unfortunately we can only offer this if you bought the book directly from us, but even if you didn't, please let us know your problem and we'll do all we can to ensure your supplier matches our commitment to you. After all, you are our ultimate customer.

We further promise to handle your orders with speed, efficiency and impressive politeness.

You can order further copies of this book, or any of our other titles, from our secure website, www.whitelionpress.com.

If you prefer, you can order by email, orders@whitelionpress.com.

Tiny Essentials of Fundraising

by Neil Sloggie
Softback, 57 pp. ISBN 0-9518971-5-2

All you really need to know about fundraising, in one tiny book.

Join Kate, an inquisitive and ambitious new recruit to the fundraising profession, as she sets out to uncover what really matters in her chosen career by visiting and asking three seasoned practitioners. Like Kate you'll see as much to avoid as to emulate in the first two encounters but you'll be reassured and inspired as, in her final meeting, Kate discovers an organisation that has really thought through its fundraising strategy and approach, and shares with her – and you – the essential secrets of fundraising success.

'A simple and truthful reminder of what's at the heart of effective fundraising. How I wish someone had given me this book when I was starting out all those years ago!'
Jan Chisholm, managing director, Pareto Fundraising, Australia.

'I was given a copy of the "Tiny" book in Australia and was so enamoured of the clear message it conveys that I ordered a special edition to give to more than 1,500 fundraisers and all 700 Blackbaud employees. Their reactions have been universally positive. *Tiny Essentials of Fundraising* is one of those books that make us truly envious of the author for executing such a brilliant piece of writing...'
Robert Sywolski, chief executive, Blackbaud Inc, USA.

'It's a smart idea, well-executed – how fabulous to have a bite-sized book that sums up what makes for successful fundraising in such an accessible way to both native and non-native English speakers.

'Great stuff. Thanks Neil for what must be the shortest, simplest and yet very salient contribution to the world's literature on fundraising.'
Julie Weston, UNHCR, Switzerland.

Tiny Essentials of Writing for Fundraising

by George Smith
Softback, 65 pp.
ISBN 0-9518971-6-0

'I suggest your heart would soar if –
once in a while – you received a letter
written in decent English which said
unexpected things in elegant ways,
which moved you and stirred your
emotions, which angered you or made you
proud, a letter apparently written by one individual to
another individual. For you never see these letters any more…'

If you believe that words matter then this opinionated little book
is for you. For this 'Tiny' book will change forever the way you
and your organisation communicate.

'*Tiny Essentials of Writing for Fundraising* is a refreshing – and
delightfully short – guide to the author's insights about the writer's
craft. If you're even thinking about writing fundraising letters you
can't afford not to buy this remarkable little book.'
Mal Warwick, chairman, Mal Warwick & Associates Inc, USA.

'I am a huge fan of George's blunt but refined writing, his clear and
individual voice, and his extraordinary ability to cut through the
crap – keep this wonderful little book next to your pen and pc.'
Lyndall Stein, CEO, Concern, UK.

'Smith is a self-confessed curmudgeon but nobody describes better
than he the power of words to advance your cause. The 11,149
words in this lovely book have been carefully selected and
assembled to help you write well enough to convince anyone of
anything.'
Ken Burnett, author, *The Zen of Fundraising*, UK.

Tiny Essentials of Major Gift Fundraising

by Neil Sloggie
Softback, 61 pp. ISBN 0-9518971-7-9

The natural successor to his first book, *Tiny Essentials of Fundraising*, this time Neil Sloggie tells the story of Daniel, who had never thought of asking any donor individually for money, nor of asking for more than a three-figure sum. Join him in his search to uncover the Holy Grail of major gift fundraising and learn as he did how to secure donations bigger than a house – and lots of them.

This 'Tiny' contains in their purest, most distilled form the priceless secrets of a neglected area of vast fundraising potential.

'Help is close at hand in this small gem – wise counsel, the importance of colleagues and networking, heaps of practical advice. To borrow Neil's words, "keep this one near the top of your priority pile".'
Sue-Anne Wallace, chief executive officer, Fundraising Institute-Australia.

'… a really helpful guide, especially to someone just starting out or wishing to do a quick reappraisal of their operation.'
Nick Booth, campaign director, NSPCC 'Full Stop' campaign, UK.

Tiny Essentials of an Effective Volunteer Board

by Ken Burnett
Softback, 81 pp. ISBN 0-9518971-8-7

When Warren Maxwell is suddenly propelled into the chairman's seat of the voluntary organisation on whose board he serves, he decides that his somewhat mediocre board is going to become a paragon of all that's excellent in nonprofit governance. Join him on his brief, eventful, enlightening quest to discover what makes a balanced, progressive and highly effective volunteer board.

'This excellent and very readable book is essential for every board member of a charity. I realise how much better a chair and trustee I could have been if only the book had been written 30 years earlier.'
Lord Joel Joffe, former chair of trustees, Oxfam UK and chair, The Giving Campaign, UK.

'This tiny book is a huge contribution to the literature on governing boards. Told as a compelling story, the insights and experience-based facts are woven skilfully throughout. A delight to read, the lessons fly off the page.'
Kay Sprinkel Grace, author, *Beyond Fundraising* and *The Ultimate Board Member's Book*, USA.

'This energising, readable book draws out what's really important, the true "tiny essentials". The 21 keys summarised in chapter six are the cream on the cake…'
Noerine Kaleeba, chair of trustees, ActionAid International, South Africa.

'This little book is absolutely brilliant; it's easy to read and is full of useful information on how to improve the effectiveness of trustee boards.

'I found this book to be a very informative resource. I loved the style; to have a fictional story to read certainly drove home the salient points far more than a dull, factual text could have done and I found this approach to be very warm and engaging.'
Tracy Saunders, information officer, in *Volunteering Magazine* July 2006, UK.

'In every field there are those who become the "philosophers" of their fields. Burnett is such a philosopher for the field of fundraising. He is, in essence, a "guru".

'Burnett's new book is appropriate for his status as fundraising guru since it exhibits the wisdom and in-depth thinking that is characteristic of one who is steeped in the history, philosophy, and literature of the field.'
Joanne Fritz, in a review on the website Nonprofit Charitable Orgs (part of the New York Times Group) August 2006, USA.

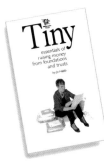

Tiny Essentials of Raising Money from Foundations and Trusts

by Jo Habib
Softback, 77 pp.
ISBN 0-9518971-9-5

Of all the world's major donors (and they are major, giving away £33 billion plus each year in the UK and USA alone), foundations and trusts may be the most pure. They have no function other than to give their money away. In *Tiny Essentials of Raising Money from Foundations and Trusts*, Jo Habib shows you with precision how to get your share.

'This book brings clarity to a world that is often apparently obscure and will help anyone understand the steps that need to be taken when approaching others for money. Written clearly and simply it will be invaluable both to the novice and to experienced old hands who think they really understand their target market. It is definitely essential reading.'
Julia Unwin, consultant and author, *The Grant-Making Tango*, UK.

'This is an encyclopaedia on fundraising from foundations and trusts packed into a tiny book. Jo Habib covers everything a new fundraiser will need to know, with admirable clarity, thoroughness and authority. Experienced fundraisers should also refer to this splendid guide, using it as a check list against which to review their own practice.'
David Carrington, consultant, UK.

Tiny Essentials of Monthly Committed Giving

by Harvey McKinnon
Softback, 70 pp. ISBN-13: 978-0-
9553993-0-5; ISBN-10: 0-9553993-0-0

This book clearly describes the secrets of
committed giving, what they are and
what they require. In an entertaining,
readable yet practical way the author
shares his insights, experience and
wisdom. You can start by benefiting
from this simple yet superbly effective
fundraising proposition in not much longer than
the 60 minutes or so it will take you to read this book.

'I read this "Tiny book" on the bus and made heads turn by laughing
out loud several times. It is easy to read, easy to understand and
will be easy to use since the 43 best ideas are summed up at the
end. Veteran fundraiser Harvey McKinnon even gives you the
answers to convince your mule of a boss that it is time to try
monthly giving, now.'
Joan Flanagan, author, *Successful Fundraising*, USA.

'Everyone has time to read a tiny book and after you read this one,
you'll be able to raise lots more money for your cause through
setting up a monthly donor program. This is one of the best uses of
an hour that I can think of.'
Rosemary Oliver, development director, Amnesty International, Canada.

'Harvey McKinnon's latest book is a kind of bedtime story for
sleepless adults – those who run financially-strapped nonprofits. If
you read it tonight, you'll sleep more peacefully. Tomorrow, you'll
start raising more money.'
Andy Robinson, author, *Big Gifts for Small Groups and Grassroots Grants*,
USA.

'This tiny guide has given philanthropy a huge gift. McKinnon's
entertaining style whilst sharing his formidable fundraising skills is in
itself an act of selfless generosity.'
Lelei LeLaulu, president, Counterpart International; chairman,
Foundation of the Peoples of the South Pacific, Canada.

Free Degrees: How to fund your own education without debt

by Lyndi Smith
Softback, 96pp.
ISBN 978-0-9553993-1-2

Your initial investment: £6.95.
Your potential return: up to £26.000.

Contrary to what many believe, education doesn't have to come at a price. Anyone can raise the funds necessary to pay their way through academic life, without getting into debt.

Without any prior experience, former drama student Lyndi Smith constructed a fundraising campaign that raised over £26,000. In Free Degrees Lyndi explains what it takes to raise money to pay for education start to finish.

'Sound and inspiring advice, as welcome to the penniless student as to the penniless actor. Bravo!'
Emma Thompson, Oscar-winning actress and screenwriter, UK.

'… really useful… astute, entertaining and very, very helpful. It offers first-class advice… Lyndi Smith makes fundraising sound like having fun.'
Professor Susan Bassnett, pro-vice chancellor and professor of comparative literature, University of Warwick, UK.

'… a life saver for teenagers about to launch into higher education – and their cash-strapped parents. Lyndi, you could be saving us thousands of pounds. Thank you.'
Jane Fricker, parent, UK.

The Zen of Fundraising

by Ken Burnett
Published by Jossey-Bass Inc in
association with The White Lion Press
Limited. Softback, 169 pp. ISBN 978-
0-7879-8314-7

If all that has ever been said and
written about the art and science of
fundraising could be distilled down to
just what really matters there would
be only a small number of true gems
deserving of the description
'nuggets of information'.

Ken Burnett has identified and defined 89 such nuggets that he
presents here as *The Zen of Fundraising* – a fun-to-read, one-of-
a-kind look into what makes donors tick and, more importantly,
what makes them give.

'Ken Burnett knows what donors want and how fundraisers can
provide it. *The Zen of Fundraising* illustrates simple yet hard-earned
lessons through which fundraisers can engage their donors as real
partners, raising more money than ever. But to succeed, fundraisers
need to aspire to greater levels of communication and donor
engagement. This books shows us how.'
Chuck Longfield, founder and CEO, Target Software Inc, USA.

'The refreshingly brief principles provide inspiration and learning to
anyone striving for exceptional fundraising practice.'
Nicci Dent, director of fundraising, Médecins sans Frontières, Australia.

'A gentle blend of humour, personal experiences and practical
examples (but underpinned by pure steel), this book makes the
most compelling case yet for thinking about donor relationships.'
Adrian Sargeant, adjunct professor of philanthropy, Indiana University
Center on Philanthropy, USA.

Relationship Fundraising: A Donor-based Approach to the Business of Raising Money (second edition)

by Ken Burnett
Published by Jossey-Bass Inc in association with The White Lion Press Limited. Hardback, 384 pp. ISBN 0-7879-6089-6

Ken Burnett has completely revised and updated his classic book *Relationship Fundraising*. Filled with illustrative case examples, donor profiles and more than 200 action points, this ground-breaking book shows fundraisers how to:

• Implement creative approaches to relationship-building fundraising.

• Avoid common fundraising errors and pitfalls.

• Apply the vital ingredients for fundraising success.

• Build good relationships with donors through marketing.

• Achieve a greater understanding of donors.

• Communicate effectively with donors – using direct mail, the press, television, the telephone, face-to-face contact, and more.

• Prepare for the challenges of twenty-first century fundraising.

'Not since Harold Seymour's classic, *Designs for Fund Raising*, has a book of this magnitude come along.

'Ken Burnett's updated and expanded work, *Relationship Fundraising*, just may be the book to which fundraising professionals turn for the next several decades.

'It is as brilliant as it is heartfelt, as simple as it is eloquent.'
Jerry Cianciolo, *The Compleat Professional's Library, Contributions Magazine*, USA.

'Ken Burnett's observations, insights and practical tips for building and sustaining relationships are superb. Highly readable, this book is a solid mix of sound theory and pragmatic application.'
Kay Sprinkel Grace, author, *Beyond Fund Raising*; co-author *High Impact Philanthropy*, USA.

'This is the book that sets the agenda for fundraising communications in the twenty-first century. Engaging, inspiring, and thought-provoking, *Relationship Fundraising* is based on the unique 25-year experience of one of the world's most respected fundraisers.'

Bernard Ross, director, The Management Centre, UK; co-author, *Breakthrough Thinking for Nonprofit Organizations.*

Friends for Life: Relationship Fundraising in Practice

by Ken Burnett
Hardback, 599 pp.
ISBN 0-9518971-2-8

Amid the widespread acclaim that greeted the 1992 publication of Ken Burnett's *Relationship Fundraising* was one persistent qualified comment. Essentially the question was 'relationship fundraising sounds very attractive, but will it help us raise more money?'

In this accessible and entertaining sequel, Ken Burnett describes how relationship fundraising is working in a wide variety of organisations in the USA, Canada and the United Kingdom. Their stories provide the answer: a loud and resounding 'yes!'

But the ideas and experiences described in this book will do much more than just help fundraisers raise more money. They will show them how to develop and maintain strong, healthy, mutually beneficial relationships with their donors; relationships that will enable them to make friends for life.

The sequel to *Relationship Fundraising* first appeared in 1996, to international acclaim.

'I'm an enthusiastic fan of Ken Burnett's approach to building friends for life. His new book builds on the practical, common-sense approach to donor development he is famous for advocating.

'Great examples, an easy read – I highly recommend *Friends for Life: Relationship Fundraising in Practice*.'
Dr Judith E Nichols, CFRE, author and consultant, USA.

'*Friends for Life* is a witty, readable tour of donor-think from both sides of the Atlantic and brings together a unique collection of experiences and anecdotes from many world-class fundraisers. *Relationship Fundraising* is already a classic throughout the world and this sequel is sure to have a similar impact.'
Jennie Thompson, consultant and co-founder of Craver, Mathews, Smith and Company, USA.

'The Botton Village case history is riveting. Its lessons have a relevance beyond fundraising. This is what direct marketing should always be, but so seldom is.'
Graeme McCorkell, author and consultant, UK.

Asking Properly: The Art of Creative Fundraising

by George Smith
Hardback, 220 pp.
ISBN 0-9518971-1-X

You will never read a book quite like this. George Smith tears open the conventional wisdom of fundraising creativity and so changes the rules for an entire trade. This book is irreverent, funny, savagely critical and genuinely inspiring, often on the same page.

Asking Properly is almost certainly the most authoritative book ever written about the creative aspects of fundraising. It is likely to remain a key text for years to come.

The author offers a profound analysis of donor motivation and is critical of the extent to which charities take their supporters for granted. But this book is no mere commentary on current practice – it offers a comprehensive checklist on how to optimise the creative presentation of the fundraising message. How to write, design, use direct mail, press advertising, broadcast media and the telephone, how to think in terms of fundraising products… the whole gallery of creativity and media is surveyed and assessed, with hundreds of examples of fundraising campaigns from around the world illustrating the need to 'ask properly'.

The book will prove invaluable to anyone involved in the fundraising process. It is provocative, entertaining and, above all, highly instructive. Read it, apply its lessons and it must enable you to raise more money.

'This book will become a classic. It's not just inspirational and a great read, there's a practical benefit on every page. When you apply George Smith's secrets you can hardly fail to improve your fundraising.'
Harvey McKinnon, president, Harvey McKinnon Associates, Canada.

'It's typically George Smith: wise, uncompromising, devastatingly critical of poor fundraising, brilliantly illustrative of what is good, full of ideas, funny, marvellously written – and exceptionally good value. In short, *Asking Properly* is one of those very few books you will keep for life.'
Pierre-Bernard Le Bas, head of fundraising, UNHCR, Switzerland.